Common Sense Revisited

"We the people are the rightful masters of both Congress and the Courts, not to overthrow the Constitution but to overthrow the men who would pervert the Constitution."

– Abraham Lincoln

Common Sense Revisited

How The Left Has Bamboozled America

John A. Mennella

Florida

Common Sense Revisited

Tiger Storm Press
1391 NW St Lucie West Blvd, Suite 247
Port St Lucie, FL 34986
TigerStormPress.com

This publication is designed to provide accurate and authoritative information regarding the subject matter covered. It is sold with the understanding that the publisher is not engaged in rendering legal, accounting, medical or other professional services.

ISBN-13: 978-1734575705

Library of Congress Control Number: 2020902581

Published in the United States of America

Dedication

I would like to say thank you to the following people, and dedicate this book to them:

My Father, Gerard Mennella and my Uncle John Schrade, two men whom I looked up to as a child, and whose footsteps I followed in when I enlisted in the United States Navy. Their guidance and encouragement led me to the decision to enlist and ultimately shaped the course of my life. I would not have become the man I am today if not for their encouragement. I would also like to thank the rest of my family, who have always supported me through good and bad times and have stood by me through it all. Special thank you to my Mother, Marida Mennella, and my Aunt A.

To my dear friend David Rosenthal who wrote one of the forwards to this book. David has been a mentor to me, and his knowledge and experiences, which he gladly shared with me on many occasions, helped shaped my passion in the quest for knowledge.

To David Webb, one of my closet friends and a true patriot who served his country proudly, and continues to give his time and efforts into bringing awareness to current events and daily issues, and all the while donating large amounts of his time to give back to veterans organizations.

To my Nephew Mario Starace, who spent many nights on the phone with me, acting as a sounding board while I passed my thoughts about this book onto him. He even provided me with some of the material that is in this book, which can be seen as one reads through the chapters.

To the Late Bob Grant, who I had the great pleasure of developing a friendship with toward the later part of his life. I recall a day I sat in his kitchen having pizza and a glass of wine, while I presented to him, my thoughts on current events. It was very surreal to be sitting in the kitchen of such a distinguished and intelligent man, while I offered him my worldly views, as he remained completely engaged and interested giving me every confidence that he felt as though I legitimately had something to offer him. This is the man who was the first media personality to interview Ronald Reagan when he first came onto the presidential circuit, and here I am garnishing his full attention. That was another one of those pivotal moments in shaping who I have become.

I would like to thank all of the brave men and women that I served with in the U.S. Navy, especially Sam Caltagerone and Jay Shoen, and all of the brave men and women I served with during my law enforcement career, particularly Dave Ganung, Steve and Jason Walrond, Khalil Hasan, Joe Walker, and Matt Stambuli.

To all the friends I have made over the years in the political realm. And to all my social media friends whose ingenious points of view and brilliant logic when combating the lunacy of the left, encouraged me to write this book.

To Michael Brue, Charles Posess, Julie Phillips, Mario Taormina, and the KW Family. The incredible power that you and KW provide when it comes to increasing mind set and breaking through ceilings, is unequivocal. The programs, the training and the coaching provided in this organization are truly priceless. There are no words to describe the culture of KW. Their motto of God, Family, Business truly leaves me speechless. And a special thanks to Gary Keller for having the vision to put this whole thing together.

To my friend and coach Keith Dean. Thank you for always being there, not only for me but for everyone at this market center, whether they are in productivity coaching or not. You are truly a student of Zig Zigler. I'll see you in Tuscany brother.

To Deb Doherty, another dear friend from KW who is the CEO and founder of a Veteran's organization by the name of DDS4VETS. Her passion to help veterans, especially disabled vets is truly inspiring. Thank you, Deb, for everything you do for our brave vets and thank you for appointing me Director of Operations for this great organization. It is truly an honor.

To my dear friend Fabrizio Bavonia, a true giver of all of himself. He is one of the most incredible first responders I have ever known. A Paramedic, Nurse, EMT, and Police Officer, he was there during 9/11 and should be very proud of all of his accomplishments. His book **"Gone But Not Forgotten, a Tribute to Voices Not Heard,"** is a testament to the man he is and the level of concern he has for mankind. A highly recommended read.

To my Publisher, Keith Dougherty from Tiger Storm Press. Thank you for keeping in touch and making this work. I appreciate your diligence and persistence in finding a path to make this happen.

And lastly to the American People without whom, I would have no purpose in writing this book. I wrote this for all of you in the hope that it will open the eyes of all of us, help expose the blatant corruption and hypocrisy that is so prevalent with the Elite in Washington, the Elite in Hollywood, and the Main Stream Media.

"The only thing necessary for the triumph of evil is for good men to do nothing."

–Edmund Burke

Table of Contents

Foreword

Fall, 2009. The event was a Town Hall. The venue was The East Brunswick, NJ Senior Center. The topic was Obamacare. The featured speaker was Congressman Rush Holt (D) NJ-12.

The room was full. Several hundred Constituents of all ages and political stripes were in that room on that chilly Saturday afternoon. Congressman Holt, frequently referred to as a Rocket Scientist was attempting to explain the features and benefits of Obamacare to a room full of Constituents, many of whom did not necessarily agree. The Congressman brought several so-called experts to help support and explain Obamacare.

I was seated near the front of the room. A loud, clear, strong voice rose from the audience assembled behind me. The room silenced. That voice challenged the statements the Congressman and the experts were making. It was clear to many in that room that the Congressman was having difficulty answering an array of simple, fair and reasonable questions. The event concluded and the crowd quickly dispersed.

Fast forward several months later at the Middlesex County Fair, I recognized that familiar face walking by. That was the person who challenged Congressman Holt at that Town Hall months before. I introduced myself and acknowledged him for having stepped up, for challenging the Congressman on key points for answers, explanations and for voicing his opinions. That was the beginning of what became a strong friendship.

Obamacare represented about 1/7 of the US Economy. As we learned more about Obamacare, John and I made it our business to pay close attention to the proposed and ever changing Obamacare plan. We attended Holt's Town Halls as they occurred throughout our Congressional District. Rep Holt came to know John and assumed John would ask relevant and tough questions. Attempting to avoid John's questions, the Congressman made it his business that his Aides instructed on-site Law Enforcement to be on-the-ready to remove or silence John from the venue.

John Mennella is a Patriot, a Student of the Constitution, a Student of History. John has good instincts and sound judgement. John sees through the clutter and noise. John served his Nation when he enlisted in the US Navy. At the conclusion of his Naval career, John served in Law Enforcement having been assigned to an array of challenging, difficult and occasionally dangerous cases.

John continues to stay in-the-game on top of the news, national events, and the political debate. He expanded his relationships with many top-of-mind politicians and commentators at CPAC, talk radio, and other media channels.

Common Sense Revisited is a precis of just that... common sense. Nowadays when listening to so-called elected leaders, politicians, judges, the media, Hollywood and elsewhere, one has to wonder whatever happened to common sense? What are they thinking? Why? All too often their thinking and actions defy logic. Assuming that elected officials have the best interests of their Constituents or our Nation top-of-mind can be a fool's errand.

John Mennella shares his observations, insights, and opinions in Common Sense Revisited.

David G. Rosenthal

David G. Rosenthal is a businessman, educator, and entrepreneur. David was part of a team at Webcraft Technologies. He served as an Advisory Board Member as well as an Adjunct Instructor at the New York University College of Graphic Communications, Management and Technology Masters Program. He is an advocate for Conservative causes.

Preface

John Mennella is a friend, but the bias of friendship does not exclude the ability to fairly assess someone. He has always stood out in his actions, public or private, as someone who prefers and acts in a manner that supports what is right from what is wrong.

His service to the nation and the military and the community and law enforcement is more than a chosen path and the reflection of who he is. Men and women with a similar approach to life took risks sometimes risking everything, and our country was founded.

John is an example of this, and he is correct that we need such men and women today in order to relight the fires of freedom.

Common Sense Revisited begins with poignant humor and takes a historical look at how we arrived at this point in time. One measure of a good book is that it engages you whether agreement is present or not.

In his book, Common Sense Revisited, John takes you down the path of critical thinking and asks that you think for yourself not what others would wish of you. Sometimes frank and harsh speech is needed. Many on the opposite side politically, who may oppose conservative thought, should remember that all speech is protected under the Constitution and the Bill of Rights, the legal DNA for our country.

In order to live up to the promise in our Declaration of Independence and the many twists and turns and evolution of America as she struggles always to be a more perfect union, we as a people have to apply and maintain common sense.

We should revisit common sense and here is your guide.

David Webb, Webb Media, LLC
SiriusXM Patriot 125 | Fox Nation Host | Fox News Contributor | The Hill Columnist

CHAPTER 1
Obituary for Common Sense

Some years ago, I came across, as it is referred to, Obituary for Common Sense. It has stuck with me for many years, and as I sit here watching the world around me crumble with lunacy, intolerance, and the inability to reason for one's self, I find myself remiss at the notion of keeping the thoughts in my head to myself. So, let me begin with the Obituary for Common Sense, and then I will continue from there:

Today we mourn the passing of a beloved friend: Common Sense. He lived a long life but died from a broken heart (technically: cardiac arrest). No one knows for sure how old he was since his birth records were long ago lost in bureaucratic red tape.

He selflessly devoted his life to service in homes, schools, businesses — and yes, even in the government — helping folks have rewarding lives, and getting jobs done while minimizing fanfare and foolishness.

He will be remembered as having cultivated such valued lessons as to know when to come in from the rain, why the early bird gets the worm, that life isn't always fair, and maybe it was my fault.

Common Sense lived by simple and sound financial policies: Don't spend more than you earn, Waste not want not, A penny saved is a penny earned, and so forth.

Mr. Sense was a tireless advocate for what used to be (in the old days) sage advice, like: Those who don't learn from history are doomed to repeat it, two wrongs don't make a right, and Actions speak louder than words.

He was also big on promoting effective parenting strategies like: the adults are in charge (not the kids), and the three R's (Responsibility, Respect, and Resourcefulness) are the most important lessons to be taught children.

In his day Little League actually had tryouts, and not everyone made the team. Those who didn't had to learn to deal with disappointment. Imagine that! Some students weren't as smart as others, so they received poor grades. Horrors! And the idea of a parent bailing him out if he broke the law was unheard of. They actually sided with the law!

Common Sense survived such cultural and educational trends as body piercing, new math and instant messaging. For decades, petty rules, silly laws and frivolous lawsuits held little impact on him. But his health started to decline when he became infected with the wide-spread Do anything, just for the sake of doing something virus. And in later years his subsequently compromised immune system proved no match for the ravages of rampant irrational regulations.

For instance, his health rapidly deteriorated when schools implemented and then mindlessly administered numerous zero tolerance policies: a six year old boy was charged with sexual harassment for kissing a classmate, a teenager was suspended for taking a swig of mouthwash after lunch, and a teacher fired for reprimanding an unruly student.

It declined even further when schools had to get parental consent to administer aspirin to a female student but could not inform a parent when the same student was pregnant or wanted an abortion. And to make sure that they were part of the problem, parents attacked teachers for doing the job they themselves failed to do in disciplining their unruly children.

Common Sense started losing the will to live as the Ten Commandments became contraband, churches became businesses, criminals received better treatment than their victims, and federal judges stuck their noses in everything from Boy Scouts to professional sports.

Common Sense took a beating when he couldn't defend himself from a burglar in his own home, as the burglar could have sued him for assault.

Then there was a woman who couldn't grasp the concept that a steaming cup of coffee was hot and was awarded a huge settlement for her own careless small spill on her lap. And smokers who indulged in three packs a day for 40 years, surprisingly got lung cancer, and then sued the tobacco company. Hearing these and similar other sad stories caused Common Sense severe distress.

As the end neared, Common Sense drifted in and out of consciousness, but was inadvisably kept informed of new irrational energy related regulations, like Renewable Portfolio Standards. When he was subsequently informed that "environmental" organizations like the Sierra Club were behind this profound pillaging of the environment Common Sense died of sudden cardiac arrest.

Mr. Sense was preceded in death by his parents: Truth and Trust, his wife: Discretion, his daughter: Responsibility; and his two sons: Diligence and Reason.

He is survived by three stepbrothers: What's in it for me, I know My rights, and I'm a Victim.

Not many attended his funeral because, so few realized he had departed. It wasn't covered by the media, no doubt due to their guilt about their complacency in bringing about his demise.

If you still remember Common Sense, please pass this on. If not, join the majority and do nothing. (Maybe, like Mark Twain, we'll be lucky enough to find that the reports of his death were greatly exaggerated.)

Now some of you may have come across this at some point in time, and this may indeed refresh your recollection of this very poignant writing, and yet some of you may be reading this for the very first time. Either way, this will serve as the foundation for the rest of this book, and the hope is that it will be the catalyst in breaking the hypnotic state that has been cast upon the masses by the Washington Elite, Hollywood Elite, and the Main Stream media.

As Thomas Paine used the original "Common Sense" as a method to open the eyes of the colonists to expose the tyranny of King George III of the United Kingdom, so shall this book be used in modern times to expose the self-evident truth that escapes the masses.

It is the author's contention that most, if not every problem that is occurring in the United States today, is due to the inability to apply common sense principals to everyday life. The inability to apply common sense to any given situation is the direct causation of bad behavior, and the justification of that behavior for any one particular individual in justifying that behavior, simply because that particular person is entitled, or is better than, or above others. So, the person may know in their heart, and in their intellect, that a behavior is wrong, but it is ok because, in their mind, the rules do not apply to them, only to everyone else. A very dear friend of mine once told me that we need to do the right thing because it is the right thing to do. Throughout this book, I will point out specific examples of legislation that have been passed, statements that have been made, behavior that has been excused, all due to the lack of common sense.

I will bring you to step by step, point by point through historical facts, and clearly show how simple everything is when we take that fictional red pill and wake from our slumber. I will use people's own statements to point out their hypocrisy, use examples from movies as analogies to make it impossible not to see the comparisons, and I will offer my view on legitimate common sense solutions, which I believe will go a long way, in not only solving many of the problems that we are currently experiencing in this country, but it will also go a long way toward unifying this country like never before.

To do this I must point out some uncomfortable facts, which in and of themselves may seem that I support a particular political party. Although I have historically supported the Republican party, I firmly believe that in the postmodern era, lines of the two parties have been blurred and there is not much difference in how they do business.

I have compiled all the information readily available and placed them into a forum in which everyone can see the truth for themselves once and for all. For those of you who are truly interested in unplugging from the Matrix, finally, in one place, the information has been compiled. It's up to you to take the red pill.

CHAPTER 2
The Right Side of History

I must point out that my historical support of the Republican Party stems from what the party itself has historically stood for, verses what the Democratic Party has historically stood for. So, to do that, let me illustrate a talking point that has been widely accepted as a fact, however when utilizing common sense principles, one realizes that it is one of the most illogical concepts ever devised. It has been said and accepted by the masses that the Republican party is a group of old white men who only care about the rich vote and that the Democratic Party is this great group of people who care about the poor vote, the little guy.

Let us analyze this statement. If we are willing to accept this absurdity as a premise, then logic (common sense), would dictate that it would behoove the Republican Party to ensure that as many people become rich as possible, so that the party itself can secure a larger voting base. If we then accept that as a premise, then once again, logic will dictate that it would behoove the Democratic Party to ensure that as many people stay poor as possible, to secure that voting block.

From this example alone, if we accept these points as facts, then, it will behoove the masses to get behind the Republican Party without question. Can you start to see how this one premise alone is absurd and has gone a long way in shaping people's thought processes inaccurately?

Now let us look at the Democratic Party, a party consisting of rich white people, and what they have been able to convince the masses of. They have convinced the masses that the reason people are poor is because of other rich white people. Are we starting to see the picture?

I have seen things on social media where people are asked very basic and simple questions, such as what party did Abraham Lincoln belong to, and many people think it is the Democratic Party. It is so apparent that there has been a big and unfortunately, a successful movement to rewrite history. Let me use this platform to correct some of the historical distortions that I believe is also a contributing factor in this ideological split that has become pervasive in our culture.

Abraham Lincoln was the first Republican President. As a matter of fact, he fundamentally did not believe in the servitude of man. Through his leadership and persistence, the Emancipation Proclamation was passed, yet somehow through revisionist history, that fact has gotten lost. In order to get it passed he had to cajole and make deals with a handful of Democratic Congressman who otherwise would have stayed behind their party line and the bill would not have passed.

It has been easy in recent years to blame everything on white privilege and talk about the mistreatment of black people in America. Now don't get me wrong, there have been some horrendous atrocities, however, just for the historical record, to point out once again just how much revisionist history there has been, the first person in America to own a slave was a black man by the name of Anthony Johnson.[1]

The Democratic Party, the party dominant in the South, created Jim Crow laws, and somehow, again, due to revisionist history, the Republicans are blamed for Jim Crow.

The Democratic Party is the party that created the KKK. In fact, many democratic politicians and judges throughout the years have previously been associated with the KKK in one form or the other.

Former Senator from West Virginia, Robert Byrd, a person whom Hillary Clinton professes to be her mentor, was, in fact, the Grand Master of the KKK.

FDR appointed a Supreme Court Justice by the name of Hugo Black, who just happened to be a member of the KKK and had a deep hatred for the Catholic Church.

The Democratic Party unanimously voted against the passage of the Civil Rights Act with the same zealous and absurd excuses that they now voted against the new Tax reform bill. In fact, Nancy Pelosi, who once said that congress had to pass Obama Care so Congress could see what was in it, now says that the tax bill is the worst piece of legislation ever to come across the Congressional Floor. The hypocrisy is overwhelming.[2]

CHAPTER 3
The Historical Case for Common Sense

The American Revolutionary War, although a 'radical' departure from their previous world ruled by kings, would usher in the context and groundwork for conservatism and the rule of common sense. The leaders of the American Revolution believed that no one man can be trusted with absolute power. The founders believed in this so heavily that even the United States government was given such limited power in its infancy due to its significant checks and balances. These checks and balances enabled the people of the United States to go about their business and day to day lives without any interruption or misrepresentation from their government. Thomas Sowell compares the American Revolution to what he calls the 'constrained vision' which is the idea that people, while deserving of freedoms and negative liberties, must realize the moral limitations inherent in mankind.

Adam Smith also recognized the limitations of mankind and attempted to examine how certain inevitable trade-offs could affect moral limitations. Thomas Sowell writes, "Smith attempted to determine how the moral and social benefits desired could be produced in the most efficient way, within that constraint.[3]" Here

Smith is approaching the limited scope of mankind's morality from a pragmatic and conservative view that admits human faults and seeks to maximize the potential of man, given his constraints. Sowell also points out that "… a society cannot function humanely, if at all when each person acts as if his little finger is more important than the lives of a hundred million other human beings."[3] It is imperative to note that trade-offs are unavoidable and that there is no perfect solution to any one human issue.

Adam Smith would place a large emphasis on trade-offs and using the inevitability of trade-offs to get a man to work for himself. Sowell describes this as "… a system of moral incentives, a set of trade-offs rather than a real solution by changing man. One of the hallmarks of the constrained vision is that it deals in trade-offs rather than solutions."[3] Smith is arguing that it does not make economical or any moral sense to throw all power behind any one individual man or entity and instead, there needs to be reciprocity. Thomas Sowell recognizes this phenomenon as the 'unconstrained vision'.

The unconstrained vision begins to argue that although a man in a state of nature prefers to be selfish, once society reaches a certain threshold and the majority hold vast amounts of wealth, the nature of man can change. Sowell points out William Godwin's words, "Men are capable, no doubt, of preferring an inferior interest of their own to a superior interest of others; but this preference arises out from a combination of circumstances and is not the necessary and invariable law of our nature. [3]" Godwin is admitting that man in a state of nature may be inclined to be selfish, but that nature is not the law of man throughout all of man's circumstances.

Edmund Burke disagrees with Godwin on the nature of man stating, "We cannot change the nature of things and of men – but must act upon them as best we can."[3] Once again, the pragmatism from the conservative outlook is able to recognize the reality that surrounds even those within high society as Edmund Burke was. Burke was able to see that what man truly is deep down, cannot and will not be changed, but that does not mean conservatism argues that man ought to act on primal instincts, but instead recognize them and try to make the absolute best moral judgement that we can, given the inevitable trade-offs examined by Adam Smith.

CHAPTER 4
A Limited Approach

The following was written by my nephew as an assignment in college as though he was writing a letter to former President Barack Obama to encourage the former president to hire him:

The United States government today plays a major role in the economy of the nation and that is why I believe there are so many economic problems facing the American people. To reduce the economic chokehold on the American people, a more limited and yet incisive economic and political plan is an absolute necessity. In any democratic society, healthy debate is the best way to achieve not only a legitimate solution but a common goal. Sitting here in front of you today and understanding what your economic philosophies have been up to this point, I have to believe that you and I would differ in our approaches. I humbly submit my plan to you with the best of intentions to aid you in finding the best possible solution to this country's economic situation.

The American economy is set up so that the free market can shift in any direction at any moment, leaving room for the government to step in and try to steer the market. This philosophy is known as Keynesian economics and it has never worked. It did not work for Woodrow Wilson, Franklin D. Roosevelt and it is not working for you, Mr. President. In the past few years, the United States economy has seen two percent growth with an inflation rate of two percent. This means that this country has not seen growth in years. What does this mean for the American people? Stagnation has been known to lead to unemployment, resulting in poverty and an overall larger welfare state.

I believe that for my plan to work, the 16th amendment must be repealed through our process of a two-thirds vote. This will be difficult to achieve due to the amount of power the amendment gives politicians through the income tax. Due to this exorbitant amount of economic power received by the members of congress, the income tax must be removed. The solution is a flat tax of twenty percent across every American. This flat tax will ensure that every person is participating and contributing to the nation no matter how much they can contribute. This will incentivize people to work harder and motivate themselves to achieve greater goals for their families and loved ones.

It has been said if you give a man a fish, he may eat for a day. However, if you teach a man how to fish, he may eat for a lifetime. The current economic and political systems do not facilitate this and as a result, we have killed his spirit, pride and self determination to strive for the American Dream. The current system is set up to gain votes and nothing more. When you continually hand someone breadcrumbs to survive, he will never have the courage to strive for more and will continue to vote for the person handing out breadcrumbs. In effect, we have a system where our government is spoon feeding people with arsenic and they are swallowing with a smile. The solution is to get back to the philosophy of teaching a person how to fish instead of handing them a check each month. Let the people earn their capital through a hard day's work. This will bring the pride and sense of accomplishment that is necessary for human existence.

To see these ideas come to fruition, we must get away from Keynesian economic principles and implement the plans that worked for Harding and Coolidge, John F. Kennedy and Ronald Reagan. To accomplish this, we are going to lower taxes and cut spending. While your stimulus plan of "priming the pump" has the intention to help the American people, I believe that pulling back on spending will give the market the opportunity it needs to see profitable growth without the hindrance of the inevitable inflation that your stimulus plan ensures. Furthermore, we currently have the highest corporate tax rate in the world, and it is no surprise that unemployment is so high when taking into account those who have given up hope and those underemployed. Targeting corporations is a red herring and although they may cut a check, it does not come from their bottom line.

When any politician plays hero to the masses by villainizing the corporations, it makes for nothing more than a sound bite and an attempt at votes. The reality is that the corporation will maintain their bottom line. They will do this by laying off workers and increase unemployment, or they will move to a foreign country with a more reliable corporate tax rate, also increasing the unemployment rate in the United States. The most likely result of the high corporate tax is a translation of the cost to the consumer. This does not mean that the government should do nothing in this case, we should be lowering the corporate tax rate to incentivize the creation of jobs for Americans and quality goods and services at fair prices, once again for the benefit of all Americans.

Sir, I sit here with the utmost respect for what you have attempted to accomplish. I submit to you, in an effort to show you that you are an intellectually honest man, it has been tried utilizing your philosophies and yet to date I do not believe we have achieved what you set out to. I ask you here and now, to give my plan a chance to flourish. Hire me, and you will not be disappointed, you will find your legacy to be the president that saved the economy of the United States.

Since this was written, just look at the difference in the economy of President Trump compared to former President Obama, simply by utilizing common sense.

CHAPTER 5
Playing Politics

This is how I see things from my perspective, with, what I believe are eyes wide open, unplugged from the Matrix:

You will see someone like Harry Reid get on TV and tell everyone in America how horrible John Boehner and all the Republicans are, and he really isn't wrong. Then you will see John Boehner get on TV and tell the American Public how horrible Harry Reid and all the Democrats are, and he really isn't wrong either. Then, while you as a Democrat and your neighbor as a Republican began to argue vehemently, both of these men will go into the Congressional Lounge and smoke cigars and drink scotch and laugh at us for buying into their nonsense as they continue to pick our pockets.

Regulation after regulation, law after law simply to justify their existence. How can anyone go on TV with a straight face and tell the American public that Congress is working very hard to get a bill through? Tax reform, 30 years in the making, and it is so difficult that it takes a whole year to achieve. No, it is not that complicated, but as long as "The Honorable" congress person tells you they are working hard for you, we blindly and willingly accept that and walk away feeling good about our elected officials. Why? Think about this.

The U.S. tax code is over 80,000 pages. Does common sense not dictate that no one can actually know what its contents are? Why are we so willing to accept this? Because our elected officials know better than us? Because they are so much more in the know than we are? Why do we accept this without question? And this question can be applied to any topic.

Every time an incident happens involving a shooting, some law maker uses it as a platform to show they care, and they are going to be the one to "fix the problem." Well, first, you cannot legislate morality. And second, the very laws they would have their constituency support, already exist. All they are doing is bloviating for the cameras, counting on the short-term memories of the masses. "My constituents will not remember the 32 previous times I have made these statements, so I will look like a hero to them, and get re-elected with ease."

Everything done in Congress is designed with a cleverly crafted title to entice you but is nothing more than a red herring. Don't believe it? Okay, let's start with health care reform, also known as *The Affordable Care Act.* The name itself is misleading. In this country, there is no health care problem. There is an insurance problem, however, they do not title it insurance reform. And why does reform of any type necessitate the need for a 2000-page bill? Solutions for this problem have been laid out time and time again. They have been short, sweet, and to the point, but that does not fit into the agenda of what law makers truly want. To confuse the American public, mislead them into thinking that the task is so Herculean that only they can achieve it, and figure a way for them to profit from it in the end.

So, what could have been done to fix the problem with insurance? Well, people have laid out the solutions time and time again, only for the media to mislead the masses, claiming that no other plan is being put out there on the table. How many times have we heard from people who truly know the fix, that there are a number of very easy ways to fix this problem?

Allow the free market to do, what the free market does and open up the purchase of insurance over state lines. This would necessarily create competition, and force prices down.

Allow for individual health savings accounts. This would allow for the policy to be attached to the person, not the company they work for.

Have true tort reform. This would cut down on frivolous lawsuits. Have a condition in this provision that would force legal fees to be paid by any person proven to have filed a frivolous suit, and in doing so, it would lower the premiums for medical malpractice. But of course, insurance companies don't want this, and neither do law makers who benefit from this to some degree, either in favors or in monetary kickbacks. And before any law makers fain being offended by that statement, give it a rest. Just look at someone like John Conyers who has supposedly been paying off mistresses with a slush fund created from taxpayer monies.[4]

Allow the doctors to determine the tests needed for their patients, not the insurance companies. Let's get back to where the relationship is between the doctors and their patients, not with the insurance companies as middlemen.

These solutions are simple, cut and dry, and probably require no more than a couple of dozen pages, yet we will accept the current bill, crafted by a man, Johnathan Grubber, who openly admits the bill was a fraud and was only able to be passed because the American public is stupid.[5,6]

All of this information is out there to be viewed by anyone who wishes, yet we fight amongst ourselves, devoid of common sense, while our law makers hoodwink us over and over again and we allow it with smiles on our faces. Why?

CHAPTER 6
Controlled Speech

Now let us tie in and expound on a point I made earlier. The clever and misleading way our law makers play on words in an attempt to make a regulation or law sound like it is something that would benefit the masses, yet, if one were to look under the surface, they would discover that this "Great law," was, in fact, nothing more than another attempt at taking away freedoms, put more money into their pocket and all while lulling us to sleep by making us think that this bill or that bill is in the best interest for us. So, let's list a few of these cleverly titled pieces of legislation/politically invented phrases:

Fairness Doctrine
Health Care Reform
Net Neutrality
Undocumented Worker
African American
Pro-Choice (Chapter 7)

Starting with the "Fairness Doctrine." Again, a misnomer created by crafty people who count on the American public to keep themselves uninformed and rely on interpretations from people who are disingenuous. In short, the "Fairness Doctrine" ensures equal time

24

for radio hosts who have points of view from both sides of the political aisle. It sounds fair, if I have a conservative talk show that has a variety of sponsorships and I have 3 hours a day and cater to a listening audience of 20 million people which will keep my sponsors happy, then a liberal host must get the same number of hours. On the surface it sounds "fair", right? However, if the liberal host only has 100,000 listeners and the sponsors pull out, and the show goes off the air, then so shall the conservative host have to go off the air. What exactly is fair about that? But if one challenges this absurdity, then they are attacked as being unsympathetic, unfair, evil or any slew of negative attacks in an attempt to silence the person trying to point out the truth.

Speaking to the health care issue as "addressed" by the Affordable Care Act. There is no health care problem in this country, there is an insurance problem. Once again, the title is misleading and a play on words. And again, all the slander comes out against anyone who disagrees, solely for the purpose of silencing the truth.

Net Neutrality is designed so the "little guy" goes out of business and the corporations' benefit. This was an Obama pet project, and again if you disagree with it, you are evil and a proponent of big corporations, and don't care about the little guy. This is what is told to the masses, yet the complete opposite is true. Those who disagree with Net neutrality, are the ones who are looking out for the little guy. Another sleight of hand by the left.[7,8]

The people on the left side of the aisle, the Nancy Pelosi's, Harry Reid's, and John Conyers' of the world, will go out of their way, in an attempt to demonize anyone who challenges their points of view. Sadly, they know very well that the ideas that they are putting out to their constituents are inaccurate at best, and more appropriately, flat out lies. As an example, once again, I must point out the carefully thought out terminology the left uses to sell their lies and demonize anyone who sees through them.

Many use the term, undocumented worker. We have been carefully manipulated and brain washed over the years to a point that we, as a society, largely accept the term. Those who don't are labeled racists, simply, in an attempt to shut those people up. If they utilized the correct and legal term, Illegal Alien, then the argument is over before it starts. The only reason they insist on using the term undocumented worker, is for political expediency, with the ultimate goal of obtaining votes.

The left's argument is completely devoid of common sense. If, as a society, we all truly understood that someone came here illegally, we would just not accept it. However, if we soften the term and say that these are just poor people trying to make a better life for themselves, then magically it becomes acceptable to sneak over the border. There are several problems with this. First, the left instantly makes this a Latin/Hispanic argument. No one is targeting that demographic. Anyone, including extremists looking to do harm to this country, can sneak over the same border. Why is this so hard a concept to grasp. Additionally, allowing people to sneak over the border illegally and doing nothing about it trivializes the people who came into this country the correct way and built a life for themselves.

The mantra of building a wall is labeled racist if we do it, yet Mexico has a wall on their southern border and no one seems to mind. In addition to having a wall, if you sneak over the border illegally into Mexico, they will put you in prison for that. If you find yourselves feeling sorry for people who come here illegally, then stop and ask yourself, if it was so important to come here, why can't it be done legally? We'll let you in if you do it correctly. For those of you who stand by the argument that removing an illegal who is already here, is cruel and breaks up a family, well, I say again, use common sense. Do we apply that same argument to an illegal or for that matter someone here legally, or born here, that commits a crime and is convicted to serve time in prison? Are we not breaking up that home? Do we let that person go for the same reasoning that the left is so aptly willing to use as a defense to prevent someone from being deported? As the owner of Gino's Philadelphia Cheese Steaks once said, "calling an illegal alien, an undocumented worker, is like calling a drug dealer, an unlicensed pharmacist."

I would like to point out another misnomer the elite has conveniently forced on us over the years, that we now, without any question or thought, have made it a part of our daily vocabulary. Over the years the elite, and left leaning people, have made many terms used in our language today, something that we have to feel uncomfortable to use. They have made common sense a thing of the past, and terms and words that have absolutely no ill meaning to them, something we should hang our heads in shame, should we use them. One of those terms, which in my opinion, not only is an absolutely incorrect "politically correct" term, but it also is racist in its foundation, and fails to allow cultural pride in an entire race of people. What is that term, and why do I bring this up? The term is African American.

In the spirit of this book, let us unplug from the Matrix, wake up, and allow ourselves to use our brains and think for ourselves. When someone refers to themselves as an Italian American, an Irish American, a German American, or even an African American to allow people to know where their heritage originates from, there is no problem with that. However, in the current political climate of our country, we do not use the term African American to explain heritage, we use it to describe the color of someone's skin. To me, it implies a subtle suggestion that being black is something to be ashamed of. Think about it, what exactly is wrong with saying someone is black or white. There is no shame in either of those things. But more importantly, and to further illustrate this point, let us truly break down the term.

Anyone with black skin in this country will instinctually be referred to as African American. If two people are having a conversation, and one of those people is referring to a black male or black female standing 100 feet away, the description would be "the African American lady or African American man" standing on the corner. But what if the person standing on the corner was from Jamaica or Haiti? That person would have been inaccurately described because they would be Jamaican American or Haitian American. What if the person standing on the corner is, in fact, African, but here legally on a student visa? Our default term would be to refer to that person as African American, however, that person is in fact, not American at all, they are just simply African. What if we are speaking with a white person from Africa, and they came to America and became a citizen? They would, in fact, be an African American, but no one would refer to them as an African American, simply because they are white, when in fact, it would be more appropriate to refer to that person as African American than the Jamaican or Haitian man or woman that came to the U.S. and became citizens. Because again, in either of those scenarios, in no universe would they be African American.

Imagine for a minute that a black family from Africa migrated to Italy 500 years ago. They adopted the culture, language, food, history, etc. Fifty years ago, a faction of that family left Italy and migrated to America. They became Citizens of the United States of America. Would they in actuality be African American or Italian American? We know how they would be described, but it is my contention that under these circumstances, this family is actually Italian American.

Utilizing the common sense and logic I have laid out; can you now ask yourself what the underlying reasoning was to create this term? It is my contention that is was cleverly crafted in an attempt, and quite successfully, to make the word black when talking about the color of someone's skin, a pejorative. Something that one should feel very uncomfortable saying. Why? Are you getting it yet? Yes, to control us, get us fighting amongst ourselves over that three-legged chair, (pages 39-40), so we take our eyes off the ball of what they, the elite are actually doing to us.

CHAPTER 7
The Treason of the Left

Let's look at housing projects. This is the darling of the Democratic party and the Elitists that believe that minorities are beneath them. They wish to be kept away from their neighborhoods and place them into poorer urban neighborhoods. And then these same elitists and Democrats turn around and successfully brain wash the American Public into thinking that it has been the Republican Party that has been their demise.

This same liberal mindset has condemned minorities to a life of complacency, killed their self-respect and self-determination by placing them into one social program after the other. The Leftists and Elitists have the poor and minorities alike on Section 8 housing, food stamps, and have kept them in low wage jobs by design. This is spoon feeding them arsenic and convincing them to take that arsenic with a smile on their faces. They then proceed to turn around and convince the masses that they are the people who are actually trying to help them escape that life, while proponents of common sense like myself and many other conservatives are the people who are the root cause of their poverty and distress. Do you see now how this is

Voldemort convincing everyone that Harry Potter and Dumbledore are the bad guys, when in fact it is Voldemort?

Look at Margaret Sanger, she created Planned Parenthood and is most famously known for her racist rants, likening black people to weeds that need to be exterminated. Why do you think that most of the Planned Parenthood clinics are in minority neighborhoods? And make no mistake about it, Planned Parenthood is nothing more than a government funded abortion clinic. So, let us talk about abortion and what it has done to this country.

Just like every other misnomer the left and the elitists concoct, let us examine the terms of pro-life vs. pro-choice. When you convince an entire nation that the term pro-choice is the actual acceptable term to use when addressing women's rights, once again, we have allowed ourselves to be brainwashed, to be plugged into the Matrix. So, let us break this down, using logic and common sense.

Let us first address the concept of "pro-choice." The term in and of itself is misleading, because of those who support abortion and label the supporting of abortion as pro-choice, pushing forward the notion that a woman has a right to do what she wants, are the first people that lose their minds when a woman's choice is to keep the baby. If a woman is on the fence of what to do and decides to keep the baby, is this their "choice?" Yet this does not fit into the pro-choice agenda.

The term "pro-choice" fails to consider what the choice of the baby would be, to live or to die. The left makes the argument that begins and ends with a woman's rights, and when those of us who oppose the murdering of a baby, stand up and fight for the rights of the baby, we are labeled misogynists who do not care about women. This is nonsensical, and quite frankly, a flat out lie and the left knows it, but they count on their slander to silence any opposition. If the term was more aptly labeled as pro-murder, instead of pro-choice, it would be less tolerated in our culture, and people would begin to promote personal responsibility rather than a "no consequence" ideology. In addition, for those of you who swear by the argument of a woman's right to choose, what about the female babies being aborted? If your only concern is the right of a woman, then does not that little girl have rights as well?

I assert that those who have resisted this concept that having an abortion is tantamount to murder, do so because they have incorrectly allowed themselves to believe that life begins at birth, rather than conception. If life begins at birth, then murder is not being committed, but if life begins at conception, it is. No one wants to admit that they are murdering, so human nature is such that one must believe that life begins at birth if they are to accept abortion.

Let us examine this notion of life beginning at birth vs. conception. If someone has a red crayon in their left hand and a blue crayon in their right hand, and they take the two, place them in a pot, put that pot onto the stove, and turn the flame on; as the crayons melt and combine into one another, molecularly you have wax.

So, if there is a human male that is 100% human DNA, and a human female that is 100% human DNA, and the two combine, at the point of that combination you have 100% human DNA. There is no getting around that, so at that point, you have life. If you end that life, what have you done? Look deep inside yourselves, unplug from the Matrix, use your common sense, and answer the question for yourselves. Before those of you who will try to make the argument that the same people who are against abortion, are for the death penalty, use your common sense, we are talking about terminating the life of an innocent baby vs. executing the life of an evil monster that has committed a heinous crime. I am sorry, but that is just apples and oranges.

Former Pennsylvania Senator and Presidential Candidate Rick Santorum once said in a debate when running for President some years ago, that in this country rape is not a crime that carries a death sentence, so in this country, we cannot kill the monster who commits the heinous act of rape, but we can kill the innocent product of that rape. Senator Santorum was 100% correct, yet the left has convinced us, that this is acceptable. Does your head hurt yet?

And here yet another point of logic and common sense pertaining to abortion. Had Barrack Obama had his way while serving as a Senator in Illinois, there would have been a law that allowed for a baby born alive during a botched abortion, to be killed, because the intent was to abort that baby. This legislation is the slippery slope that not only leads to the killing of babies but the disproportionate killing of black babies, as planned by Margaret Sanger, the darling of the left, in order to "exterminate the weeds" to eradicate the black race. This is the treason of the left. So, you get pregnant and decide to have an abortion, you go into the clinic with this intention, and the baby is born alive. At this point, you decide to keep the baby, and 15 years later, this child annoys you to no end, and you kill him or her. You are arrested for murder. Is your defense now that your intention 15 years ago was to abort the child, so you killing this child now is in fact not murder, but just following up on the intent you had 15 years earlier? And since abortion is legal, you have committed no crime? Do you see how liberalism is truly a mental disorder? And look where this thinking has now gotten us. The left now uses the term post-birth abortion. This is now a good thing in their book. They celebrate this passage of legislation. Folks, it is my contention that abortion is murder at any stage, but for those who can see their way to disagreeing with that, would you be so brazen to disagree that post-birth abortion is, in fact, actual murder? Is this now what we accept as a nation.

In all of the points that I have laid out here showing how the left, and the elitists use a negative campaign of name calling when someone does not agree with them, let me quote Socrates, **He said that when the argument is lost, slander becomes the tool of the loser.**

It is a very uncomfortable feeling to be labeled a racist, a homophobe, a misogynist, and they know it. But again, this is a trick of the left. Be strong and do not capitulate to their trickery. This is one of the biggest reasons this country is in the mess it is in. They push and push and push with lunacy, and we take the position that their position is so nonsensical that we should just ignore it and say nothing. Well, we have said nothing for so long that their lunacy has now become a pervasive way of thinking. A good majority of people fall into this trap.

Another cleverly devised trick of the left is the notion that one cannot talk religion or politics at the dinner table or at a bar. These are the exact places one should talk about these things. Honest healthy dialogue is the best way to exchange ideas and keep everyone informed. This notion is by design, because if no one talks about any of these things amongst themselves, then the leftist agenda can be pushed through without any challenge from anyone because there would be no one person informed enough to challenge them, let alone know what to challenge.[9]

CHAPTER 8
Just Entertain Us

How have we gotten to the point where we have become so conditioned that we accept absurdity as a standard and never question anything that has been sold to us? We don't even think to question things that, should we stop for a second and ponder it, we would have such clarity, that the elite could no longer successfully lull us to sleep.

How do they accomplish this? To properly explain this, I would once again like to use an analogy by citing a scene from a 1974 movie, The Taking of Pelham 123. The movie starred Walter Matthau as a cop investigating a train robbery in NYC. Nearing the end of the movie, Walter Matthau and his partner are following up leads of possible suspects and one of the suspects works as a toll booth collector at the Verrazano Bridge. The scene was shot on location, or at least some of the footage of that scene was, and as Walter Matthau and his partner approached the toll booths, you can clearly see the cost of the toll was 25 cents. The cost of the toll last I checked was 17 dollars. So, how does this have anything to do with the point I make pertaining to the progressive formula?

Imagine if the toll is 25 cents in 1974 and 50 cents in 1975 and 95 cents in 1980, and it goes up exponentially over 40 years until it reaches 17 dollars. No one notices, no one complains, no one is outraged, because this has been done very deliberately and slowly over this stretch of time. If the cost of that toll was 25 cents today, and 17 dollars tomorrow, no one would stand for it, no one would allow it, and no one would pay it. Yet we allow ourselves to be brow beat and might I say, plugged into the Matrix, without question.

It is really no different from the concept of placing a lobster into a lukewarm pot of water and heating it up slowly until the lobsters are cooked or placing the live lobster into a boiling pot. You know the rest.

How is it that we got to this point of complete acceptance of mindless terminology that is solely used to control us and keep us at each other's throats arguing about nonsensical things. Well, I will get to that in a moment but let me first point out another method used by our puppeteers, to keep us arguing over two nonsensical points, rather than discussing the actual point to the conversation, in other words, they keep us from discussing what should actually be discussed.

Imagine for a minute that you and another person are arguing over sitting down in the blue chair. You tell that other person to sit in the blue chair and that person tells you that they do not like the color blue. So, the two of you argue this point for hours and walk away angry and dissatisfied for not getting the other person to see your point of view. However, you and this other person never discussed the fact that the chair has only 3 legs and they could not sit down anyway. See, this is the trick of the elite to keep us distracted from the real issues, and to keep us pitted against one another.

A perfect example in an attempt to unplug everyone from the Matrix; I am sure most of you have watched the Harry Potter series. Just look at 2 of the movies, in particular, *The Order of the Phoenix* and *The Deathly Hallows Part 2*. In The Order of the Phoenix, the bad guy, Voldemort, has been able to convince the masses that he is in fact not back, when we know, as viewers, that he is. He has been able to install members of his order into high level positions in the ministry and the School of Hogwarts. He even has the press launching a negative campaign against Harry Potter and Dumbledore.

In *The Deathly Hallows Part 2*, Voldemort uses fear in an attempt to get the masses to attack Harry Potter, knowing full well that Harry is the only person who can beat him. He is terrified of Harry and tried to get good, decent people to do his bidding because, at the end of the day, he is no match for Harry. If you do not think that in this case, and in many others, the lines of art and life have not been blurred, you are still sleeping.

Look at the movie Captain America, you learn in this series that Hydra has infiltrated Shield. Again, on the surface, an absurd reference to a movie, however, I have come to realize that sometimes it is easier for people to make a correlation with visual aids that they are more comfortable with. It is hard for people to accept that everything they have been told to believe in their whole lives may very well be wrong. When we watch these movies, we all get angry that the bad guys were able to weave their way through the system and accomplish what they have been able to accomplish. We all have an innate sense of right over wrong, and we are all relieved in the end when the good guy wins. Why do we continue to allow our elected leaders to get away with what they have gotten away with over the past 100 years or so?

If we were a part of the movie, knowing what we know as viewers, we would not allow Hydra to get away with it, or Voldemort to achieve what he did. Yet, like Voldemort being able to convince the masses that Harry Potter was the bad guy, people like Hillary Clinton have been able to convince the masses that legitimate people who are trying to honestly help, are the bad guys. Why do we continue to allow this?

Even a block buster movie such as the Star Wars franchise has that same good vs. evil theme. And in that movie the Emperor/Sith Lord always attempts to downplay the good people, attempts to convince them that they have no chance at succeeding and control everyone with fear. This brings to mind an old saying by Edmond Burke... "All it takes for evil to triumph is for good men to do nothing."

The problem is that all of these movies have the same subtle theme, as evil begins to lose its hold on the masses it steps up the fear and propaganda against the good guy. So how do we now tie this into real life, real common-sense principals. Well for decades now we have had politicians on both sides of the aisle do whatever it took to win even at the expense of detriment to the country. And once they win, they fall right into the stream of the Washington Elite and learn very quickly how to answer with the old D.C. dip and twirl. To illustrate this, I have selected a scene from an old comedy movie "The Distinguished Gentleman."[10]

I am going to keep this theme of utilizing clips from movies or actual statements from politicians because I understand the human condition and I am very well aware of how life imitates art and art imitates life. And yes, I am very well aware that the scenes from movies are just that, scenes from movies, however, it is my contention that these scenes are not all that far off from the reality that takes place in D.C.[11]

I assert that I have shown time and time again throughout this book that we have lost our way as a nation with regard to common sense, and the causation of this, I have shown, is due to a slow progressive course of conditioning and brainwashing over a long period of time. During the time it took to bring this nation to where it is today, we have clearly forgotten the initial intent of our founders. When the U.S. Constitution was finalized, Benjamin Franklin was approached and asked what sort of government the delegates had created, to which he replied, **a republic, if you can keep it**. However, over the years we have lost the meaning of what we were given. Our government was not merely founded with the idea of consent of the people, it is dependent upon an active and informed constituency in order for this form of government to survive.

It is my contention, that in fact the elite have slowly, progressively, and deliberately lulled a population to sleep, plugged them into the Matrix, so to speak, and transformed this government into one that is no longer governed by the will of the people, it is governed by elitists who are unhinged, and will do anything to protect their nest eggs. This is exactly how and why both political parties resist and demonize a man like Donald Trump (The Harry Potter and Dumbledore of our time). They are the true Voldemort, and it is time everyone opens their eyes, unplugs from the Matrix, and recognizes what is truly going on.

To illustrate how we have lost our way, I will use another example from a scene of a TV show. This time, it is a clip from Star Trek, in an episode named "Omega Glory." In this episode, a parallel world, identical to Earth, was unable to escape the war that we avoided, and the Asians took over the world. For many years we fought back, until such time as we were once again a free nation. In this scene, Captain Kirk explains the true meaning of the words in the Constitution, and how it was created by the people, for the people. It is very poignant and worth watching. I believe that this scene will enlighten many of you, if not all of you.[12]

After watching this scene, perhaps this may refresh one's recollection of the importance of this document and the flag itself and how it is a symbol of our pride and freedom. The argument that the flag itself gives us the right to disrespect it is a circular and convoluted argument and flawed on its face. The Supreme Court covering the burning of a flag under free speech is offensive and cowardly, and quite frankly, in my opinion, destructive, as it allows us as a nation to head down that slippery slope of moving further and further away from the original intent. At the same time, this makes it acceptable to find flaws with a nation that has been the leader in fighting and defeating tyranny throughout the world. That is our legacy, not one of imperialism and colonization as the elitist will do everything they can to convince you of.

Even the recent disrespect within the ranks of the NFL with regard to kneeling for our nation's anthem is justified under a false argument. It has been maintained that it is the right of these players to protest as covered under the first amendment. However, this is a flawed argument in as much as the Constitution and its amendments protect us against infringement from the government. It does not give us the right to do whatever we want at our place of employment.

From an economic standpoint, kneeling for the flag is illogical and quite frankly, stupid. A CEO of any company is or should be concerned with the bottom line. The actions of these players have alienated at least 50% of the viewers and have resulted in a decline in revenue. Even from the player's perspectives, their million-dollar contracts rely on profits made through concessions, parking, purchasing of team paraphernalia, sponsors, etc. If you offend 50%

of your clientele, how can you fail to understand that you are directly hurting your bottom line?

Why did these protests happen? Let's break it down. First, I would like to say that from the perspective of the players, they may very well have been doing this with 100% good intentions, truly passionate about their cause, sincerely believing in the oppression that still exists in this country. Given that belief, I certainly understand their passion, however, as I have pointed out throughout this book, it is my belief that their passion is created from misinformation conveyed to many through corrupt politicians, untruthful media, only concerned about selling stories regardless of the accuracy of those stories and other elitists dead set on manipulating the masses. As I explained earlier using the example of how the political leaders play us against one another, so do all other elitists. Let's go back to common sense. A group of people who are in a complete different economic class than most of us, have convinced the rest of us, who have a lot more in common with each other than they do with that elitist class that has created this narrative, that oppression of minorities still exists on a level that is just as bad today, as it was 100 years ago.

Let us examine this absurdity. Let us start with the most obvious. If this country has such institutionalized racism, then how on God's Green Earth can one explain the ability to have elected a Black President 2 terms. Regardless of what the elitists have been able to successfully sell to the masses, Barrack Obama does not get elected without White America. Yet any time someone disagreed with his policies or his ideologies, they were instantly labeled a racist. A strategy right out of Sol Alinsky's Rules for Radicals. Years ago, I heard a caller on the Rush Limbaugh Radio show make the most brilliant point pertaining to these absurd allegations of racism, simply for disagreeing with an ideology. This caller said that it was not the black half of Barrack Obama that we do not like, we actually like that half of him; it is the white elitist, European, socialist half of him that we do not like. Let that sink in!

Herman Caine, when running for office once said something to the effect that this is the only country that has the ability to correct its mistakes and grow from them. The idea that the elite has convinced a whole segment of society that they are owed something because of the wrongs of the past is so disingenuous and so harmful to that segment of the population, I cannot begin to list the absurdities. Moreover, the people pushing forth this narrative, know that they are lying, however, they lie for the exact reason I have cited in this book many times over. They lie to keep us at odds with one another, so we do not pay attention to what they are doing, while they continue to profit and line their own pockets off our blood sweat and tears.

Somehow, they have convinced a whole segment of the population, who have never been slaves, that other people, who have never been slave owners, somehow owe them something. Does no one recognize the sleight of hand being levied against all of us? The real question is, why have we all failed to recognize what they are doing to us, again spoon feeding us arsenic, and we take it with a smile on our faces.

As I have pointed out throughout this book, the agenda of the left has always been and continues to be "We know how to live your life for you better then you do, we know what's best for you." In doing so, we should be thankful for their wisdom and will to "make our lives better." There are many examples throughout this book illustrating this, but in lieu of recent events, I would like to give you, what I think, is a perfect example of this. In the movie Infinity Wars, there is a scene where Ebony Maw first makes contact with Iron Man and Dr. Strange. Pay particular attention to the 1:32 mark of the following video. Iron Man and Dr. Strange are told to "hear me and rejoice, you are about to die at the hands of the children of Thanos, be thankful that your meaningless lives will now contribute to the balance…" Although this is nothing more than a scene in a movie, it so perfectly illustrates the mentality of the left. Their agenda, their belief system is the only way. You are too stupid to know what's good for you.[13]

In recent events what can I possibly compare this scene to real life. We have a President who has been duly elected by the will of the people, who have grown tired of the shenanigans that occur daily in Washington. He has been getting things done like no other president and things have been improving on a daily basis with his policies. However, because he operates outside of the "D.C. norm" of doing things, and he is not utilizing a play book that has been proven ineffective over the past 50 years, there is a faction of the entrenched that want to push forth the idea that he is unfit. So much so, that the press will omit facts, flat out lie, and now the possibility that someone in the White House is leaking information. WHY? Because we are too stupid to know what's good for us, but they know better.

So, like in the movie, I should smile and be thankful that they are here to kill me, I should shake their hand and kneel down before them, so should I be thankful for all of these people who are subversive to this President, so that he can go, and we can get another D.C. insider who will do nothing but raise taxes, enact absurd regulations, and continue to steal our hard earned money, keep us asleep and keep us in the collective. And if that were to happen, we should be thankful, shake their hands, and get down on our knees.

CHAPTER 9
Truth

Let us discuss current events and get back to the trickery and debauchery that the evil levees against the good. As I stated earlier, many of the elite attempt to demonize Donald Trump, a man who is outside of the D.C. Elite and feared because of it. For this, he is made out to be a villain, and we have already used the Harry Potter comparison, so let us get down to the brass tacks of the matter. Liz Crokin is an Award-winning author, a seasoned journalist and an advocate for sex crime victims. Liz began her journey at the University of Iowa where she received a bachelor's in journalism and political science. I came across this in an E-mail sent to me and I believe this says it all. She writes the following:

'Trump Does The Unthinkable' by Liz Crokin

Donald Trump is a racist, bigot, sexist, xenophobe, anti-Semitic and Islamophobe -- did I miss anything?.....Oh Right he is also deplorable. The left and the media launch these hideous kinds of attacks at Trump every day; yet, nothing could be further from the truth about the real estate mogul.

As an entertainment journalist, I've had the opportunity to cover Trump for over a decade, and in all my years covering him I've never heard anything negative about the man until he announced he was running for president. Keep in mind, I got paid a lot of money to dig up dirt on celebrities like Trump for a living so a scandalous story on the famous billionaire could've potentially sold a lot of magazines and would've been a Huge feather in my cap.

Instead, I found that he doesn't drink alcohol or do drugs, he's a hardworking businessman.

On top of that, he's one of the most generous celebrities in the world with a heart filled with more gold than his $100 million New York penthouse.

Since the media has failed so miserably at reporting the truth about Trump, I decided to put together some of the acts of kindness he's committed over three decades which has gone virtually unnoticed or fallen on deaf ears.

• In 1986, Trump prevented the foreclosure of Annabell Hill's family farm after her husband committed suicide. Trump personally phoned down to the auction to stop the sale of her home and offered the widow money. Trump decided to take action after he saw Hill's pleas for help in news reports.

• *In 1988, a commercial airline refused to fly Andrew Ten, a sick Orthodox Jewish child with a rare illness, across the country to get medical care because he had to travel with an elaborate life-support system. His grief stricken parents contacted Trump for help and he didn't hesitate to send his own plane to take the child from Los Angeles to New York so he could get his treatment.*

• *In 1991, 200 Marines who served in Operation Desert Storm spent time at Camp Lejune in North Carolina before they were scheduled to return home to their families. However, the Marines were told that a mistake had been made and an aircraft would not be able to take them home on their scheduled departure date. When Trump got wind of this, he sent his plane to make two trips from North Carolina to Miami to safely return the Gulf War Marines to their loved ones.*

• *In 1995, a motorist stopped to help Trump after the limo he was traveling in got a flat tire. Trump asked the Good Samaritan how he could repay him for his help. All the man asked for was a bouquet of flowers for his wife. A few weeks later Trump sent the flowers with a note that read:*

We've paid off your mortgage.

• *In 1996, Trump filed a lawsuit against the city of Palm Beach, Florida, accusing the town of discriminating against his Mar-a-Lago resort club because it allowed Jews and blacks. Abraham Foxman, who was the Anti-Defamation League Director at the time, said Trump put the light on Palm Beach not on the beauty and the glitter, but on its seamier side of discrimination. Foxman also noted that Trump's charge had a trickle-down effect because other clubs followed his lead and began admitting Jews and blacks.*

• In 2000, Maury Povich featured a little girl named Megan who struggled with Brittle Bone Disease on his show and Trump happened to be watching. Trump said the little girl's story and positive attitude touched his heart. So he contacted Maury and gifted the little girl and her family with a very generous check.

• In 2008, after Jennifer Hudson's family members were tragically murdered in Chicago, Trump put the Oscar-winning actress and her family up at his Windy City hotel for free. In addition to that, Trump's security took extra measures to ensure Hudson and her family members were safe during such a difficult time.

• In 2013, New York bus driver Darnell Barton spotted a woman close to the edge of a bridge staring at traffic below as he drove by. He stopped the bus, got out and put his arm around the woman and saved her life by convincing her to not jump. When Trump heard about this story, he sent

the hero bus driver a check simply because he believed his good deed deserved to be rewarded.

• In 2014, Trump gave $25,000 to Sgt. Andrew Tahmoressi after he spent seven months in a Mexican jail for accidentally crossing the US–Mexico border. President Barack Obama couldn't even be bothered to make one phone call to assist with the United States Marine's release; however, Trump opened his pocketbook to help this serviceman get back on his feet.

• In 2016, Melissa Consin Young attended a Trump rally and tearfully thanked Trump for changing her life. She said she proudly stood on stage with Trump as Miss Wisconsin USA in 2005. However, years later she found herself struggling with an incurable illness and during her darkest days she explained that she received a handwritten letter from Trump telling her she's the bravest woman, I know. She said the opportunities that she got from Trump and his organizations ultimately provided her Mexican-American son with a full-ride to college.

• Lynne Patton, a black female executive for the Trump Organization, released a statement in 2016 defending her boss against accusations that he's a racist and a bigot. She tearfully revealed how she's struggled with substance abuse and addiction for years. Instead of kicking her to the curb, she said the Trump Organization and his entire family loyally stood by her through immensely difficult times.

Donald Trump's kindness knows no bounds and his generosity has and continues to touch the lives of people from every sex, race and religion. When Trump sees someone in need, he wants to help. Two decades ago, Oprah asked Trump in a TV interview if he'd run for president. He said: If it got so bad, I would never want to rule it out totally, because I really am tired of seeing what's happening with this country.

Trump sees that America is in need and he wants to help. How unthinkable!

On the other hand, have you ever heard of Hillary or Obama ever doing such things with their own resources?

Now that's really unthinkable! Might be worth passing on!!! Oh, by the way, Trump's annual salary as President is donated to charity...

After having read this and seeing the type of man President Trump really is, can you now start to get the picture how we are being manipulated by a terrified group of elitists that see their world collapsing, and their nest egg crumbling because we finally have someone beyond their control. Now, in the theme of this book, I would be remiss if I did not point out that the reason the elitists do this and feel they can get away with it, is because they are counting on the lack of common sense and the naivety of the masses. We cannot allow them to get away with this.

They say ignorance is bliss, and knowledge is power. I submit to you that the Democratic Plantation that still exists today, is no different now, then they were in the 1800s. Think about it, I have shown you time and time again throughout this book that the Washington Elite, the Hollywood Elite, and the Mainstream Media are all working in conjunction with one another to keep people in the dark. They distort the truth, make laws that only affect the masses, but do not apply to them, and constantly tell us how to live our lives, yet do not adhere to their own standards which they force on all of us. What is the difference between what they do now and what they did by keeping enslaved people uneducated, not allowed to read? I assure you this is done by design, and remember, a rose by any other name is still a rose. It is the same result; they just sprinkled a little sugar on top to keep everyone off guard.

Think about it, what do they do now? They give people handouts, kill their self-determination, make them think that they are doing justice, and then convince everyone that the people that are truly attempting to help them, are in fact the bad guys who want to take everything away from them. They literally keep people in the dark about their true intentions. What is so different when comparing that to preventing people to learn how to read. They are basically giving people something for nothing and convincing them to be happy about it. But, just remember, any government big enough to give you everything, is big enough to take it all away.

Our founders gave us a document in our Constitution that was like nothing ever seen before or since. It gives the power to the people and limits governmental power. Back in the 1860s, during the Lincoln days, Frederick Douglas, a former slave, who did not know how to read, was told by people that the Constitution was a flawed document. Once he taught himself to read, and took the time to read it for himself, he made the realization that the Constitution was, in fact, one of the most brilliant documents ever to have been written. So, prior to his learning to read, he was forced to rely on others to tell him what is good, and what is bad, (ignorance is bliss). But, once he was able to decide for himself, understood what had been given to us by our founders, he knew that he had been misled. (Knowledge is power.)

CHAPTER 10
Revival

I can certainly make this book thousands of pages long, as the lunacy of the left never seems to end, but I will keep it short, sweet and to the point and conclude with the following:

Where has complacency gotten us? Look where ignoring the foolishness of the left has led this nation. We now have a congresswoman who ran on a platform of supporting her people in an urban area, when she grew up in Westchester and went to Boston College to obtain a degree in economics. Whoever paid for her college education should get their money back because this woman knows nothing about economics. Now we have a 30-something year old congresswoman who tweets about the commoners, like you and I sitting in the cheap seats while she runs the nation. She knows nothing about how government works, she thinks there are three chambers of government including the Presidency, the Senate and the House. She is the exact reason why they need to put Civics back in schools.

For some reason, these people have been able to convince a whole segment of our society that socialism is the way to go, yet let me ask you if socialism is so great how come people that flee other nations, flee to the United States, and not socialistic countries. If we don't fight back against this now, we will lose our country. We are perhaps one or two elections away from doing so, we must take a stand, no longer ignore these people and their stupidity, and recognize them for the dangerous people they truly are.

For the future of our Nation, we must revive Common Sense.

Acknowledgments

About David G. Rosenthal

David G. Rosenthal is acknowledged in the Graphic Communications industry for his leadership, executive management, innovative techniques, methods, solutions, and products. David founded Shepard Communications Group, Inc., a direct marketing consulting firm. He formerly was Senior Vice President, Sales and Marketing of Webcraft Technologies serving on the firm's Executive Management Committee. He led a national sales organization serving markets throughout the United States. David is a founding principle of Optimal Fire Prevention Systems LLC. The firm developed and holds multiple patents for an innovative method for true fire prevention.

David is a graduate of the Rochester Institute of Technology. He sat on the Board of Advisors of the New York University Center for Graphic Communications Management and Technology also serving as an Adjunct Instructor in the School of Professional Studies Masters Program.

Mr. Rosenthal served on the Board of Directors of Printing Industries of America; and The Association of Graphic

Communications serving as Board Chairman. He served on the Advisory Board of e-LYNXX Corporation. David also served as a Board Member of the Graphic Communications Scholarship, Award & Career Advancement Foundation.

David is a Middlesex County New Jersey County Committeeman and sat on the East Brunswick Zoning Board of Adjustment. He was a Candidate for the Middlesex County Board of Chosen Freeholders. David was appointed by Governor Brendan Byrne to serve on the Selective Service Board also serving as Local Board Chairman.

David served in the US Army Reserve during the Vietnam Era.

About the artists and the cover

Sue Parriot and Maria de Fatima C Paiva, are two of the loveliest ladies I have ever meet. When I first came up with the idea for this cover, and thank you, Evan Maltzman, for the initial concept, I was uncertain how to get this from thought to canvass. Let me take you down that path with a brief story of how this picture became a reality.

I was on the phone one day with one of my best friends, Evan Maltzman, and we were discussing ideas for a book cover. All of a sudden Evan shouted out, "go big or go home," and continued by saying, "why don't you just have the Founding Fathers on their knees in shackles, with Pelosi and Schumer behind them. I pondered that thought for a while, and later that day I found myself waking into an art store speaking with the owner. I asked if he knew any local artists that could take on a project for a book cover. He took my name and number and assured me that he would have someone contact me.

Several days later, I received a call from Sue Parriott who informed me that her business partner, and fellow artist, Maria de Fatima C Paiva would be glad to meet with me to discuss the project. A few days later, there I was at their Art Studio ART-N-AROUND.

Expounding on Evan's idea, I explained to Sue and Maria What my vision for the cover was, and they decided to take on the project. Within two and a half weeks, and several progress meetings along the way, they came up with the cover you now see. As the picture started to take shape, I would tweak a thing or two here or there, put a silhouette of the Liberty Bell here, rearrange the order of the Founders there, what everyone would be clad in, ensuring that the picture had quite a bit of symbolism worked into it. Some of the symbolism may be obvious, and yet some not so much, so please allow me to explain the hidden meanings of this amazing picture by Sue and Maria.

As you can see the size of Independence hall circa 1776, and how it pales in size to the modern-day U.S. Capital Building. This is done intentionally to depict the image of what started out as an idea of liberty and freedom, has been overtaken by this monstrosity of tyranny. If you will notice the sky over Independence Hall, it is much clearer and brighter, and as we move halfway beyond the Liberty Bell, the sky begins to turn dark and cloudy. I think the symbolism there is obvious. Then there is the order of the Founders. I deliberately had Benjamin Franklin placed in the first position, as I wanted him to be the closest Founder to Independence Hall. The reason for this is from the story of a lady approaching Mr. Franklin shortly after the Constitution was signed. She approached him in the square of Independence Hall and asked him "Sir what have you given us?" and his reply was "Madam, we have given you a republic if you can keep it." OPINIG, I think we can all see how that is working out.

Anyway, I digress. I think the picture speaks for itself, and with a small explanation of the symbolism, Sue and Maria have done an excellent job, and I cannot thank these two ladies enough. Anyone who needs artwork done, I highly recommend reaching out to them and utilizing their talents and services.

About The Author

 At the age of 17, I chose to serve my country in the U.S. Navy. I spent 5 years in the Intelligence Community and received an honorable discharge upon completion of my enlistment.

Upon entering the civilian world, I pursued a career in law enforcement. I spent 28 years and retired as a Detective in New Jersey.

I always had a passion for politics and history, and I have been very active in the conservative movement over the past couple of decades.

I am an avid reader, who has been very fortunate over the years to have read historical books on our founders, economic books by the likes of Milton Freidman, Thomas Sowell, F.A. Hayek. I have read authors such as John C. Maxwell, Napoleon Hill, and many other personal development books, the list goes on and on. I have a deep understanding and appreciation for my contribution to my fellow man.

After the last several years, in seeing the direction this country is heading in and understanding how precious our freedom is, and how easy it is to lose, I decided to write this book in an attempt to help people change their perspective and recognize what is really going on in our country, and who the true enemy is. I hope this book serves as that proverbial "red pill," and helps everyone open their eyes to the staggering level of corruption that has been taking place for many decades.

I also hope this book serves as an awakening for all of you, and perhaps this book can put the power back into the hands of "WE THE PEOPLE," and out of the hands of the corrupt political class that has run this nation into the ground.

Works Cited

1. Encyclopediavirginia.org. (2020). Court Ruling on Anthony Johnson and His Servant (1655). [online] Available at: https://www.encyclopediavirginia.org/Court_Ruling_on_Anthony_Johnson_and_His_Servant_1655

2. FreePropaganda. (2013, May 28). Nancy Pelosi Pass the Bill to find out what's in it [Video file]. Retrieved from https://youtu.be/QV7dDSgbaQ0

3. Sowell, Thomas. A Conflict of Visions. New Delhi: Affiliated East-West, 1988. Print.

4. Rodriguez, K. (2020). Another Democrat Used Secret Congressional 'Slush Fund' to Settle Sexual Harassment Allegations. [online] Breitbart. Available at: http://www.breitbart.com/big-government/2017/12/05/another-democrat-used-secret-congressional-slush-fund-settle-sexual-harassment-allegations/

5. Avik Roy. (2014, November 12). 3 Jonathan Gruber Videos: Americans "Too Stupid to Understand" Obamacare [Video

file]. Retrieved from https://youtu.be/Adrdmmh7bMo

6. ReidBaerPoetry. (2014, December 09). Trey Gowdy SAVAGES Jonathan Gruber (VIDEO) [Video file]. Retrieved from https://youtu.be/TG7gYNE-WWs

7. Ben Shapiro. (2017, December 2). Ben Shapiro BREAKS DOWN Net Neutrality [Video file]. Retrieved from https://youtu.be/yBrZ_CPgm7o

8. StevenCrowder. (2017, December 4). NET NEUTRALITY: Why Big Corporations Support It. | Louder With Crowder [Video file]. Retrieved from https://youtu.be/G35g5HQVjpU

9. One America News Network. (2017, May 30). Planned Parenthood's worst enemy on cable television, @Liz_Wheeler [Video file]. Retrieved from https://youtu.be/ty0UYNLf25g

10. Bill Pascoe. (2009, October 7). The Distinguished Gentleman [Video file]. Retrieved from https://youtu.be/w7fBwc803CI

11. TilDeath1776 US. (2016, March 23). Hillary Clinton calls African American super predators, she's the racist. Breaking news [Video file]. Retrieved from https://youtu.be/Rj6RmDYFKKA

12. Superfluous Muse. (2016, November 8). The Omega Glory: "We the People..." - Star Trek OS, S2 E23 Gentleman [Video file]. Retrieved from https://youtu.be/5Fajy-Fy_uA

13. Subline. (2018, August 8). Ebony Maw: All Quotes (Avengers: Infinity War) [Video file]. Retrieved from https://youtu.be/94QBW-n8oE0

Made in the USA
Monee, IL
12 November 2020

47370109R00051